50 Essential Taco Tuesday Recipes

By: Kelly Johnson

Table of Contents

- Classic Beef Tacos
- Chicken Tinga Tacos
- Shrimp Tacos with Mango Salsa
- Veggie Tacos with Black Beans
- Pork Carnitas Tacos
- Spicy Fish Tacos with Slaw
- Taco Al Pastor
- Breakfast Tacos with Eggs and Bacon
- Korean BBQ Beef Tacos
- Cauliflower Tacos with Chipotle Sauce
- Turkey Taco Lettuce Wraps
- Lobster Tacos with Avocado Crema
- BBQ Chicken Tacos
- Sweet Potato and Black Bean Tacos
- Chicken Fajita Tacos
- Jerk Chicken Tacos
- Greek-Style Tacos with Tzatziki
- Chipotle Beef Tacos
- Crispy Potato Tacos
- Vegetarian Taco Salad
- Taco Stuffed Peppers
- Taco Flatbreads
- Thai Peanut Chicken Tacos
- Lentil Tacos with Avocado
- Spicy Chorizo Tacos
- Pumpkin and Black Bean Tacos
- Apple Cider Pulled Pork Tacos
- Cilantro Lime Chicken Tacos
- Tacos de Pescado (Fish Tacos)
- Quinoa Tacos with Avocado Dressing
- BBQ Jackfruit Tacos
- Buffalo Cauliflower Tacos
- Cilantro-Lime Shrimp Tacos
- Roasted Beet Tacos with Goat Cheese
- Tofu Tacos with Avocado and Lime

- Thai Shrimp Tacos with Peanut Sauce
- Spicy Beef Taco Bowl
- Italian Sausage Tacos
- Chicken Mole Tacos
- Fried Egg Tacos with Salsa Verde
- Mexican Street Corn Tacos
- Chicken Parmesan Tacos
- Grilled Vegetable Tacos
- Pineapple Salsa Chicken Tacos
- Tomato and Basil Caprese Tacos
- Creamy Chipotle Chicken Tacos
- Mexican Shrimp Cocktail Tacos
- Spicy Lentil and Kale Tacos
- BBQ Beef Brisket Tacos
- Cilantro-Lime Rice Tacos

Classic Beef Tacos

Ingredients:

- 1 lb ground beef
- 1 packet taco seasoning
- 8 taco shells
- Toppings (lettuce, cheese, salsa, sour cream)

Instructions:

1. **Cook Beef:** In a skillet over medium heat, cook ground beef until browned. Drain excess fat.
2. **Add Seasoning:** Stir in taco seasoning and follow package instructions (usually adding water and simmering for a few minutes).
3. **Assemble Tacos:** Spoon beef mixture into taco shells and add desired toppings. Serve immediately.

Chicken Tinga Tacos

Ingredients:

- 1 lb cooked chicken, shredded
- 1 can (14 oz) diced tomatoes
- 1 onion, sliced
- 1 tablespoon chipotle in adobo sauce
- Corn tortillas, for serving

Instructions:

1. **Sauté Onions:** In a skillet, sauté sliced onion until translucent.
2. **Add Chicken and Sauce:** Add shredded chicken, diced tomatoes, and chipotle sauce. Simmer for 10 minutes.
3. **Serve:** Warm corn tortillas and fill with chicken tinga mixture. Enjoy with your favorite toppings.

Shrimp Tacos with Mango Salsa

Ingredients:

- 1 lb shrimp, peeled and deveined
- 1 teaspoon chili powder
- 1 cup diced mango
- 1/4 cup red onion, diced
- Flour tortillas, for serving

Instructions:

1. **Season Shrimp:** Toss shrimp with chili powder, salt, and pepper.
2. **Cook Shrimp:** In a skillet, cook shrimp over medium heat for 2-3 minutes on each side until pink.
3. **Make Salsa:** In a bowl, combine diced mango and red onion. Serve shrimp in flour tortillas topped with mango salsa.

Veggie Tacos with Black Beans

Ingredients:

- 1 can (15 oz) black beans, drained and rinsed
- 1 bell pepper, diced
- 1 zucchini, diced
- 1 teaspoon cumin
- Corn tortillas, for serving

Instructions:

1. **Cook Veggies:** In a skillet, sauté bell pepper and zucchini until tender.
2. **Add Beans and Seasoning:** Stir in black beans and cumin, cooking until heated through.
3. **Assemble Tacos:** Serve veggie mixture in corn tortillas, adding toppings as desired.

Pork Carnitas Tacos

Ingredients:

- 2 lbs pork shoulder
- 1 onion, quartered
- 1 tablespoon cumin
- 1 tablespoon oregano
- Corn tortillas, for serving

Instructions:

1. **Slow Cook Pork:** Place pork shoulder in a slow cooker with onion, cumin, and oregano. Cook on low for 8 hours or until tender.
2. **Shred Pork:** Remove pork, shred it with two forks, and return to slow cooker to absorb juices.
3. **Serve:** Fill corn tortillas with carnitas and top with your choice of salsa, onion, or cilantro.

Spicy Fish Tacos with Slaw

Ingredients:

- 1 lb white fish (e.g., tilapia), cut into strips
- 1 tablespoon chili powder
- 2 cups cabbage slaw
- 1/4 cup mayonnaise
- Corn tortillas, for serving

Instructions:

1. **Season Fish:** Toss fish strips with chili powder, salt, and pepper.
2. **Cook Fish:** In a skillet, cook fish over medium heat for 3-4 minutes per side until flaky.
3. **Make Slaw:** In a bowl, mix cabbage slaw with mayonnaise. Serve fish in corn tortillas topped with slaw.

Taco Al Pastor

Ingredients:

- 1 lb pork loin, thinly sliced
- 1/4 cup pineapple juice
- 1 tablespoon achiote paste
- 1 onion, chopped
- Corn tortillas, for serving

Instructions:

1. **Marinate Pork:** In a bowl, combine pork, pineapple juice, and achiote paste. Marinate for at least 1 hour.
2. **Cook Pork:** In a skillet, cook marinated pork until browned and cooked through.
3. **Serve:** Fill corn tortillas with pork and top with chopped onion and fresh cilantro.

Breakfast Tacos with Eggs and Bacon

Ingredients:

- 6 eggs, beaten
- 4 strips bacon, cooked and crumbled
- 1/2 cup cheese, shredded
- 8 small tortillas
- Salsa, for serving

Instructions:

1. **Cook Eggs:** In a skillet, scramble eggs until cooked through.
2. **Combine Ingredients:** Add crumbled bacon and cheese, stirring until cheese is melted.
3. **Assemble Tacos:** Spoon egg mixture into tortillas and serve with salsa.

Korean BBQ Beef Tacos

Ingredients:

- 1 lb flank steak
- 1/4 cup soy sauce
- 2 tablespoons brown sugar
- 1 tablespoon sesame oil
- Corn tortillas, for serving

Instructions:

1. **Marinate Beef:** In a bowl, combine soy sauce, brown sugar, and sesame oil. Add flank steak and marinate for at least 30 minutes.
2. **Cook Beef:** Grill or pan-sear the steak for 5-7 minutes per side until cooked to desired doneness. Slice thinly.
3. **Serve:** Fill corn tortillas with sliced beef and top with cilantro and green onions.

Cauliflower Tacos with Chipotle Sauce

Ingredients:

- 1 head cauliflower, chopped
- 2 tablespoons olive oil
- 1 teaspoon cumin
- 1/2 cup sour cream
- 1-2 chipotle peppers in adobo, minced

Instructions:

1. **Roast Cauliflower:** Preheat oven to 425°F (220°C). Toss cauliflower with olive oil and cumin. Spread on a baking sheet and roast for 25-30 minutes until golden.
2. **Make Chipotle Sauce:** In a bowl, mix sour cream and minced chipotle peppers.
3. **Assemble Tacos:** Fill tortillas with roasted cauliflower and drizzle with chipotle sauce.

Turkey Taco Lettuce Wraps

Ingredients:

- 1 lb ground turkey
- 1 packet taco seasoning
- 8 large lettuce leaves
- Toppings (diced tomatoes, cheese, avocado)

Instructions:

1. **Cook Turkey:** In a skillet, cook ground turkey until browned. Add taco seasoning and water according to package instructions.
2. **Serve in Lettuce:** Spoon turkey mixture into lettuce leaves and top with diced tomatoes, cheese, and avocado.

Lobster Tacos with Avocado Crema

Ingredients:

- 1 lb cooked lobster meat, chopped
- 1 avocado
- 1/2 cup sour cream
- 1 lime, juiced
- Corn tortillas, for serving

Instructions:

1. **Make Avocado Crema:** In a blender, combine avocado, sour cream, and lime juice. Blend until smooth.
2. **Warm Lobster:** In a skillet, gently heat chopped lobster meat.
3. **Serve:** Fill corn tortillas with lobster and drizzle with avocado crema.

BBQ Chicken Tacos

Ingredients:

- 2 cups cooked chicken, shredded
- 1/2 cup BBQ sauce
- 8 taco shells
- Toppings (coleslaw, pickles)

Instructions:

1. **Mix Chicken and Sauce:** In a bowl, combine shredded chicken with BBQ sauce.
2. **Assemble Tacos:** Spoon BBQ chicken into taco shells and top with coleslaw and pickles.

Sweet Potato and Black Bean Tacos

Ingredients:

- 2 sweet potatoes, peeled and diced
- 1 can (15 oz) black beans, drained and rinsed
- 1 teaspoon cumin
- Corn tortillas, for serving

Instructions:

1. **Roast Sweet Potatoes:** Preheat oven to 425°F (220°C). Toss diced sweet potatoes with olive oil and cumin. Roast for 25-30 minutes until tender.
2. **Combine with Beans:** In a bowl, mix roasted sweet potatoes and black beans.
3. **Serve:** Fill corn tortillas with the mixture and top with avocado and salsa.

Chicken Fajita Tacos

Ingredients:

- 1 lb chicken breast, sliced
- 1 bell pepper, sliced
- 1 onion, sliced
- 1 tablespoon fajita seasoning
- Flour tortillas, for serving

Instructions:

1. **Cook Chicken and Veggies:** In a skillet, sauté chicken, bell pepper, and onion until chicken is cooked through and veggies are tender. Add fajita seasoning.
2. **Serve:** Fill flour tortillas with the chicken fajita mixture.

Jerk Chicken Tacos

Ingredients:

- 1 lb chicken thighs, boneless and skinless
- 2 tablespoons jerk seasoning
- 1 mango, diced
- Corn tortillas, for serving

Instructions:

1. **Marinate Chicken:** Rub chicken thighs with jerk seasoning. Let marinate for at least 30 minutes.
2. **Cook Chicken:** Grill or pan-sear chicken until cooked through. Slice thinly.
3. **Serve:** Fill corn tortillas with jerk chicken and top with diced mango.

Greek-Style Tacos with Tzatziki

Ingredients:

- 1 lb ground lamb or beef
- 1 tablespoon olive oil
- 1 teaspoon oregano
- 1 cup tzatziki sauce
- Pita or flatbreads, for serving

Instructions:

1. **Cook Meat:** In a skillet, heat olive oil and cook ground lamb or beef until browned. Stir in oregano and season with salt and pepper.
2. **Assemble Tacos:** Spoon the meat into pita or flatbreads and top with tzatziki sauce, diced tomatoes, and chopped cucumbers.

Chipotle Beef Tacos

Ingredients:

- 1 lb ground beef
- 1 tablespoon chipotle chili powder
- 8 taco shells
- Toppings (cheese, lettuce, salsa)

Instructions:

1. **Cook Beef:** In a skillet, cook ground beef over medium heat until browned. Drain excess fat.
2. **Add Chipotle:** Stir in chipotle chili powder and cook for an additional 2 minutes.
3. **Serve:** Fill taco shells with beef and your favorite toppings.

Crispy Potato Tacos

Ingredients:

- 2 large potatoes, peeled and diced
- 1 teaspoon cumin
- 8 corn tortillas
- Oil, for frying

Instructions:

1. **Cook Potatoes:** Boil diced potatoes until tender. Drain and mash slightly. Season with cumin and salt.
2. **Fry Tortillas:** In a skillet, heat oil over medium heat. Fry corn tortillas until crispy.
3. **Fill Tacos:** Fill crispy tortillas with mashed potatoes and top with salsa and avocado.

Vegetarian Taco Salad

Ingredients:

- 1 can (15 oz) black beans, drained and rinsed
- 1 cup corn kernels
- 1 bell pepper, diced
- 1 cup cherry tomatoes, halved
- Tortilla chips, for serving

Instructions:

1. **Combine Ingredients:** In a large bowl, combine black beans, corn, bell pepper, and cherry tomatoes. Season with lime juice, salt, and pepper.
2. **Serve:** Serve the salad on a bed of tortilla chips, topping with cheese and avocado if desired.

Taco Stuffed Peppers

Ingredients:

- 4 bell peppers, halved and seeded
- 1 lb ground turkey or beef
- 1 packet taco seasoning
- 1 cup cooked rice
- 1 cup cheese, shredded

Instructions:

1. **Cook Meat:** In a skillet, brown ground turkey or beef. Stir in taco seasoning and cooked rice.
2. **Stuff Peppers:** Fill bell pepper halves with the meat mixture and top with cheese.
3. **Bake:** Place stuffed peppers in a baking dish and bake at 375°F (190°C) for 25-30 minutes until peppers are tender.

Taco Flatbreads

Ingredients:

- 1 lb ground beef or turkey
- 1 packet taco seasoning
- 4 flatbreads
- Toppings (sour cream, lettuce, cheese)

Instructions:

1. **Cook Meat:** In a skillet, cook ground meat until browned. Stir in taco seasoning.
2. **Assemble Flatbreads:** Spread the meat mixture over flatbreads and top with desired toppings.
3. **Serve:** Cut into slices and serve warm.

Thai Peanut Chicken Tacos

Ingredients:

- 1 lb cooked chicken, shredded
- 1/2 cup peanut sauce
- 8 small tortillas
- Toppings (cabbage, cilantro, lime)

Instructions:

1. **Mix Chicken and Sauce:** In a bowl, combine shredded chicken with peanut sauce until well coated.
2. **Serve:** Fill tortillas with the chicken mixture and top with shredded cabbage, cilantro, and a squeeze of lime.

Lentil Tacos with Avocado

Ingredients:

- 1 cup cooked lentils
- 1 teaspoon cumin
- 1 avocado, diced
- 8 corn tortillas
- Toppings (salsa, cilantro)

Instructions:

1. **Season Lentils:** In a bowl, mix cooked lentils with cumin, salt, and pepper.
2. **Serve:** Fill corn tortillas with lentils and top with diced avocado, salsa, and cilantro.

Spicy Chorizo Tacos

Ingredients:

- 1 lb spicy chorizo sausage, casings removed
- 8 corn tortillas
- 1 cup diced onions
- Toppings (cilantro, avocado, lime)

Instructions:

1. **Cook Chorizo:** In a skillet, cook chorizo over medium heat until browned and cooked through, breaking it up with a spoon.
2. **Warm Tortillas:** Heat corn tortillas in a separate skillet until soft.
3. **Assemble Tacos:** Fill tortillas with cooked chorizo and top with diced onions, cilantro, avocado, and a squeeze of lime.

Pumpkin and Black Bean Tacos

Ingredients:

- 1 can (15 oz) pumpkin puree
- 1 can (15 oz) black beans, drained and rinsed
- 1 teaspoon cumin
- 8 corn tortillas
- Toppings (sour cream, diced avocado)

Instructions:

1. **Heat Filling:** In a saucepan, combine pumpkin puree, black beans, cumin, salt, and pepper. Heat until warm.
2. **Warm Tortillas:** Heat corn tortillas in a skillet until soft.
3. **Serve:** Fill tortillas with the pumpkin and black bean mixture and top with sour cream and diced avocado.

Apple Cider Pulled Pork Tacos

Ingredients:

- 2 lbs pork shoulder
- 1 cup apple cider
- 1 tablespoon apple cider vinegar
- 8 taco shells
- Toppings (coleslaw, pickles)

Instructions:

1. **Slow Cook Pork:** Place pork shoulder in a slow cooker. Add apple cider and vinegar. Cook on low for 8 hours or until tender. Shred with a fork.
2. **Serve:** Fill taco shells with pulled pork and top with coleslaw and pickles.

Cilantro Lime Chicken Tacos

Ingredients:

- 1 lb chicken breasts, cooked and shredded
- 1/4 cup fresh lime juice
- 1/4 cup chopped cilantro
- 8 tortillas
- Toppings (sour cream, diced tomatoes)

Instructions:

1. **Mix Chicken:** In a bowl, combine shredded chicken with lime juice, cilantro, salt, and pepper.
2. **Warm Tortillas:** Heat tortillas in a skillet until warm.
3. **Assemble Tacos:** Fill tortillas with cilantro lime chicken and top with sour cream and diced tomatoes.

Tacos de Pescado (Fish Tacos)

Ingredients:

- 1 lb white fish fillets (like cod or tilapia)
- 1 tablespoon taco seasoning
- 8 corn tortillas
- Toppings (cabbage slaw, lime crema)

Instructions:

1. **Cook Fish:** Season fish fillets with taco seasoning. Cook in a skillet until flaky and cooked through.
2. **Warm Tortillas:** Heat corn tortillas until soft.
3. **Serve:** Fill tortillas with fish and top with cabbage slaw and lime crema.

Quinoa Tacos with Avocado Dressing

Ingredients:

- 1 cup cooked quinoa
- 1 can (15 oz) black beans, drained and rinsed
- 1 avocado
- 1/4 cup Greek yogurt
- 8 corn tortillas

Instructions:

1. **Mix Filling:** In a bowl, combine cooked quinoa and black beans. Season with salt and pepper.
2. **Make Dressing:** In a blender, combine avocado, Greek yogurt, lime juice, and salt until smooth.
3. **Assemble Tacos:** Fill tortillas with quinoa mixture and drizzle with avocado dressing.

BBQ Jackfruit Tacos

Ingredients:

- 2 cans (20 oz) young green jackfruit in water or brine, drained and rinsed
- 1/2 cup BBQ sauce
- 8 taco shells
- Toppings (coleslaw, pickles)

Instructions:

1. **Prepare Jackfruit:** In a skillet, cook jackfruit until it starts to break apart. Stir in BBQ sauce and cook until heated through.
2. **Serve:** Fill taco shells with BBQ jackfruit and top with coleslaw and pickles.

Buffalo Cauliflower Tacos

Ingredients:

- 1 head cauliflower, chopped into florets
- 1/2 cup buffalo sauce
- 8 tortillas
- Toppings (blue cheese dressing, celery)

Instructions:

1. **Roast Cauliflower:** Preheat oven to 425°F (220°C). Toss cauliflower with buffalo sauce and roast for 25-30 minutes until tender.
2. **Warm Tortillas:** Heat tortillas in a skillet until warm.
3. **Serve:** Fill tortillas with buffalo cauliflower and top with blue cheese dressing and celery.

Cilantro-Lime Shrimp Tacos

Ingredients:

- 1 lb shrimp, peeled and deveined
- 1/4 cup fresh lime juice
- 1/4 cup chopped cilantro
- 8 tortillas
- Toppings (sour cream, avocado)

Instructions:

1. **Cook Shrimp:** In a skillet, cook shrimp until pink and cooked through. Add lime juice and cilantro, tossing to combine.
2. **Warm Tortillas:** Heat tortillas in a skillet until warm.
3. **Assemble Tacos:** Fill tortillas with shrimp and top with sour cream and avocado.

Roasted Beet Tacos with Goat Cheese

Ingredients:

- 2 medium beets, roasted and diced
- 8 corn tortillas
- 4 oz goat cheese, crumbled
- 1 cup arugula or spinach
- Toppings (balsamic glaze, walnuts)

Instructions:

1. **Prepare Beets:** Roast beets in the oven until tender. Allow to cool, peel, and dice.
2. **Warm Tortillas:** Heat corn tortillas in a skillet until soft.
3. **Assemble Tacos:** Fill tortillas with roasted beets, crumbled goat cheese, and arugula. Drizzle with balsamic glaze and top with walnuts.

Tofu Tacos with Avocado and Lime

Ingredients:

- 14 oz firm tofu, drained and crumbled
- 1 avocado, sliced
- 8 corn tortillas
- 1 lime, juiced
- Toppings (cilantro, salsa)

Instructions:

1. **Cook Tofu:** In a skillet, cook crumbled tofu until golden and slightly crispy. Add lime juice and season with salt.
2. **Warm Tortillas:** Heat corn tortillas until soft.
3. **Assemble Tacos:** Fill tortillas with tofu, avocado slices, and top with cilantro and salsa.

Thai Shrimp Tacos with Peanut Sauce

Ingredients:

- 1 lb shrimp, peeled and deveined
- 1/2 cup peanut sauce
- 8 corn tortillas
- Toppings (cabbage slaw, lime wedges)

Instructions:

1. **Cook Shrimp:** In a skillet, cook shrimp until pink and cooked through. Toss with peanut sauce.
2. **Warm Tortillas:** Heat corn tortillas in a skillet until warm.
3. **Serve:** Fill tortillas with shrimp and top with cabbage slaw and lime wedges.

Spicy Beef Taco Bowl

Ingredients:

- 1 lb ground beef
- 1 tablespoon taco seasoning
- 1 cup cooked rice or quinoa
- 1 can (15 oz) black beans, drained and rinsed
- Toppings (cheese, salsa, avocado)

Instructions:

1. **Cook Beef:** In a skillet, cook ground beef until browned. Add taco seasoning and cook according to package instructions.
2. **Assemble Bowl:** In bowls, layer cooked rice or quinoa, black beans, seasoned beef, and desired toppings.

Italian Sausage Tacos

Ingredients:

- 1 lb Italian sausage, casings removed
- 8 corn tortillas
- 1 cup sautéed bell peppers and onions
- Toppings (parmesan cheese, marinara sauce)

Instructions:

1. **Cook Sausage:** In a skillet, cook Italian sausage until browned and cooked through. Drain excess fat.
2. **Warm Tortillas:** Heat corn tortillas in a skillet until soft.
3. **Assemble Tacos:** Fill tortillas with sausage, sautéed peppers and onions, and top with parmesan cheese and marinara sauce.

Chicken Mole Tacos

Ingredients:

- 2 cups shredded cooked chicken
- 1/2 cup mole sauce
- 8 tortillas
- Toppings (sour cream, cilantro)

Instructions:

1. **Mix Chicken:** In a bowl, combine shredded chicken and mole sauce, heating gently.
2. **Warm Tortillas:** Heat tortillas in a skillet until warm.
3. **Serve:** Fill tortillas with chicken mole and top with sour cream and cilantro.

Fried Egg Tacos with Salsa Verde

Ingredients:

- 4 large eggs
- 8 corn tortillas
- 1/2 cup salsa verde
- Toppings (avocado, cilantro)

Instructions:

1. **Fry Eggs:** In a skillet, fry eggs to your desired doneness.
2. **Warm Tortillas:** Heat corn tortillas until soft.
3. **Assemble Tacos:** Fill tortillas with fried eggs, drizzle with salsa verde, and top with avocado and cilantro.

Mexican Street Corn Tacos

Ingredients:

- 2 cups grilled corn (or canned)
- 8 corn tortillas
- 1/4 cup mayonnaise
- 1/4 cup cotija cheese, crumbled
- Toppings (lime juice, chili powder)

Instructions:

1. **Prepare Corn:** In a bowl, mix grilled corn with mayonnaise, lime juice, and chili powder.
2. **Warm Tortillas:** Heat corn tortillas until soft.
3. **Assemble Tacos:** Fill tortillas with the corn mixture and top with cotija cheese.

Chicken Parmesan Tacos

Ingredients:

- 1 lb cooked chicken breast, shredded
- 1 cup marinara sauce
- 1 cup mozzarella cheese, shredded
- 8 flour tortillas
- Toppings (fresh basil, parmesan cheese)

Instructions:

1. **Mix Chicken:** In a bowl, combine shredded chicken and marinara sauce. Heat until warmed through.
2. **Warm Tortillas:** Heat flour tortillas in a skillet until soft.
3. **Assemble Tacos:** Fill tortillas with chicken mixture, top with mozzarella cheese, and garnish with fresh basil and parmesan cheese.

Grilled Vegetable Tacos

Ingredients:

- 2 zucchini, sliced
- 1 bell pepper, sliced
- 1 onion, sliced
- 8 corn tortillas
- Toppings (avocado, cilantro, lime)

Instructions:

1. **Grill Vegetables:** Toss vegetables with olive oil, salt, and pepper. Grill until tender.
2. **Warm Tortillas:** Heat corn tortillas in a skillet until soft.
3. **Assemble Tacos:** Fill tortillas with grilled vegetables and top with avocado, cilantro, and a squeeze of lime.

Pineapple Salsa Chicken Tacos

Ingredients:

- 1 lb cooked chicken, shredded
- 1 cup pineapple salsa
- 8 corn tortillas
- Toppings (cilantro, lime wedges)

Instructions:

1. **Mix Chicken:** In a bowl, combine shredded chicken and pineapple salsa. Heat until warmed through.
2. **Warm Tortillas:** Heat corn tortillas in a skillet until soft.
3. **Assemble Tacos:** Fill tortillas with chicken mixture and top with cilantro and lime wedges.

Tomato and Basil Caprese Tacos

Ingredients:

- 1 cup cherry tomatoes, halved
- 1 cup mozzarella balls, halved
- Fresh basil leaves
- 8 corn tortillas
- Drizzle of balsamic glaze

Instructions:

1. **Prepare Filling:** In a bowl, mix cherry tomatoes and mozzarella. Season with salt and pepper.
2. **Warm Tortillas:** Heat corn tortillas in a skillet until soft.
3. **Assemble Tacos:** Fill tortillas with tomato and mozzarella mixture, add basil leaves, and drizzle with balsamic glaze.

Creamy Chipotle Chicken Tacos

Ingredients:

- 1 lb cooked chicken, shredded
- 1/2 cup chipotle sauce
- 8 flour tortillas
- Toppings (avocado, cilantro)

Instructions:

1. **Mix Chicken:** In a bowl, combine shredded chicken and chipotle sauce. Heat until warmed through.
2. **Warm Tortillas:** Heat flour tortillas in a skillet until soft.
3. **Assemble Tacos:** Fill tortillas with chicken mixture and top with avocado and cilantro.

Mexican Shrimp Cocktail Tacos

Ingredients:

- 1 lb shrimp, cooked and chopped
- 1/2 cup cocktail sauce
- 8 corn tortillas
- Toppings (avocado, cilantro)

Instructions:

1. **Mix Shrimp:** In a bowl, combine chopped shrimp and cocktail sauce.
2. **Warm Tortillas:** Heat corn tortillas in a skillet until soft.
3. **Assemble Tacos:** Fill tortillas with shrimp mixture and top with avocado and cilantro.

Spicy Lentil and Kale Tacos

Ingredients:

- 1 cup cooked lentils
- 2 cups kale, chopped
- 8 corn tortillas
- 1 tablespoon taco seasoning
- Toppings (sour cream, salsa)

Instructions:

1. **Cook Kale:** In a skillet, sauté kale until wilted. Add cooked lentils and taco seasoning, heating through.
2. **Warm Tortillas:** Heat corn tortillas in a skillet until soft.
3. **Assemble Tacos:** Fill tortillas with lentil and kale mixture and top with sour cream and salsa.

BBQ Beef Brisket Tacos

Ingredients:

- 1 lb cooked brisket, shredded
- 1 cup BBQ sauce
- 8 corn tortillas
- Toppings (coleslaw, pickles)

Instructions:

1. **Mix Brisket:** In a bowl, combine shredded brisket and BBQ sauce. Heat until warmed through.
2. **Warm Tortillas:** Heat corn tortillas in a skillet until soft.
3. **Assemble Tacos:** Fill tortillas with brisket mixture and top with coleslaw and pickles.

Cilantro-Lime Rice Tacos

Ingredients:

- 2 cups cooked rice
- 1/4 cup cilantro, chopped
- Juice of 1 lime
- 8 corn tortillas
- Toppings (black beans, avocado)

Instructions:

1. **Mix Rice:** In a bowl, combine cooked rice with chopped cilantro and lime juice. Season with salt.
2. **Warm Tortillas:** Heat corn tortillas in a skillet until soft.
3. **Assemble Tacos:** Fill tortillas with cilantro-lime rice and top with black beans and avocado.

www.ingramcontent.com/pod-product-compliance
Lightning Source LLC
LaVergne TN
LVHW081336060526
838201LV00055B/2686